Polish Cuisine

Authentic Polish Cookbook

Lukas Procházka

Copyright © 2017 Lukas Prochazka
All rights reserved.
ISBN: 1547092890
ISBN-13: 978-1547092895

License Note

No part of this book is permitted to be reproduce in any form or by any means unless a permission is given by its author. All recipes in this book are written only for informative purpose. All readers should be advised to follow the instruction at their own risk.

About the Author

I consider myself to be very skilled cook and a good author of many cookbooks, which are now being sold worldwide. I was born in a small town in the north of Czechia. Since very young age I have been drawn to cooking. In 2012 I wrote my first internationally sold cookbook about Czech cuisine. Four years later I republished this book in improved version and since then I have kept on writing new titles. I hope you find my books to be useful and you will get inspiration from these.

For more cookbooks please visit
www.amazon.com/author/prochazkacook

Subscribe on Twitter to stay informed:
www.twitter.com/ProchazkaCook

CONTENTS

Introduction 6

Soups

Borshch 8
Czarnina, Black Soup 9
Flaki, Tripe Soup 10
Grochówka, Pea Soup 11
Chłodnik, Cold Borshch 12
Kapuśniak, Cabbage Soup 13
Kartoflanka, Potato Soup 14
Krupnik, Barley Soup 15
Rosoł, Broth with Noodles 16
Zupa Grzybowa, Mushroom Soup 17
Zupa Ogórkowa, Pickle Soup 18
Zupa Szczawiowa, Sorrel Soup 19
Zupa Tomidorowa, Tomato Soup 20
Żurek, Rye Soup 21

Main Courses

Bigos 24
Golabki, Cabbage Rolls 25
Kaczka z Jabłkami, Duck with Apples 26
Klopsiki, Polish Meatballs 27
Kotlet Mielony 29
Kotlet Schabowy 30
Łosoś Pieczony, Baked Salmon 31
Paszteciki 32
Pierogi with Cheese Filling 34
Placki Ziemniaczane, Potato Pancakes 35
Polish Goulash 36
Pyzy, Meat Stuffed Potato Dumplings 37
Zrazy 38

Desserts

Budyn, Vanilla Pudding 40
Faworki 41
Chalka, Jewish Challah 42
Kissel 43
Makoviec 44
Mazurek, Flat Cake 46
Pączki, Doughnuts 47
Sernik, Polish Cheesecake 48

Side Dishes

Ćwikla 50
Kopytka, Potato Dumplings 51
Mizeria, Cucumber Salad 52
Tłuczone Ziemniaki, Mashed Potatoes 53

Volume Conversion 54
Weights of Common Ingredients 55
Temperature Conversion 56
Length Conversion 57

About Polish Cuisine

In the Middle Ages was based on dishes made of agricultural produce, meats of wild and farm animals and fruits, herbs and local spices. It was known above all from abundant salt using and permanent presence of groats. A high calorific value of dishes and drinking the beer as a basic drink, unlike the wine spread in south and west Europe, was typical of Middle Ages Polish cuisine. A beer and a mead were most popular drink for a lot of time, but with time an expensive wine, imported mainly from Silesia and Hungary appeared.

Medieval chronicles describe Polish cuisine as very pungent, using large amounts of the meat and groats. Indeed, medieval Polish cuisine applied prodigious seasonings amounts (when compared with other countries of Europe), mainly pepper, nutmeg and juniper. Thanks to close trade relations between Poland and countries of the Orient, prices of spices were lower in Poland than in many other countries. Up to today's times mentions of aromatic, dense and very spicy Polish sauces behaved ('jucha szara' and 'jucha czerwona', nowadays unknown). Apart from that balm, the turnip and pea were common. What's interesting in the Middle Ages a flatware wasn't used at all.

If you want to try traditional Polish cuisine, stop counting your calories. Typical meals are very hearty and often contain a lot of meat. The most typical ingredients used in Polish cuisine are sauerkraut, beetroot, cucumbers, sour cream, kohlrabi, mushrooms, sausages and smoked sausage.

Bigos, Polish Stew

Soups

Kartoflanka, Potato Soup

Borshch

Yield: 6 servings

Ingredients:

1 1/2 cup sliced potatoes
1 cup of sliced beets
1 and half cup of chopped onion
3 cups of chopped red cabbage
1/4 teaspoon of fresh dill
2 tablespoons of butter
1 teaspoon of caraway seed
1 chopped celery stalk
1 sliced large carrot
1 tablespoon of cider vinegar
1 tablespoon of honey
1 cup of tomato puree
2 teaspoons of salt
Black pepper to taste

Directions:

1. Boil potatoes and beets until tender.
2. Remove potatoes and beets. Reserve stock.
3. Meanwhile melt butter in large saucepan.
4. Stir in onion, caraway seeds and salt. Fry until onion turns gold. Stir in celery, carrot and cabbage.
5. Mix in reserved stock and cook for about 10 minutes.
6. Add potatoes, beets and tomato puree.
7. Reduce heat to medium and boil for at least 30 minutes.
8. Serve the soup topped with sour cream and dill.

Czarnina, Black Soup

Yield: 8 servings

Ingredients:

1 whole duck
4 cups of duck blood
8 cups of water
2 whole garlic cloves
500g pitted prunes
1/2 cup of raisins
1 apple
1 stalk of celery
2 tablespoons of flour
1 tablespoon of sugar
1 chopped sprig of parsley
1 cup of cooking cream
5 whole allspice pieces
1 tablespoon of lemon juice
Salt

Directions:

1. Boil the whole duck, celery, parsley, allspice and garlic cloves for 1 and half hour. You can put the vegetable and spice in a cloth bag.
2. Remove vegetable and duck. Discard bones. Cut meat and return it to broth.
3. Mix in sliced prunes, raisins and chopped apples.
4. Simmer for 30 minutes.
5. Meanwhile in a medium bowl beat flour, cream and sugar.
6. Add duck blood. Mix it well.
7. Add 1/2 of hot soup stop and mix it well again.
8. Pour the mixture in the pot. Stirring in constantly and boil it for a while.
9. Serve.

Flaki, Tripe Soup

Yield: 8 servings

Ingredients:

500g beef tripes
500g pork stomachs
2 marrowbones
300g root vegetables
4 garlic cloves
1 tablespoon of flour
1 tablespoon of sweet paprika
Marjoram
Lard
Black pepper
Pinch of salt

Directions:

1. Boil tripes and stomach for 20 minutes with marrowbones in salt water.
2. Meanwhile fry diced vegetable in lard.
3. Remove tripes, stomachs and marrowbones.
4. Slice tripes and stomachs into strips and put them back.
5. Add vegetable, garlic, salt and pepper.
6. Make roux from sweet paprika and flour.
7. Add to the broth.
8. Serve with marjoram.

Grochówka, Pea Soup

Yield: 6 servings

Ingredients:

1,5l beef broth
500g pea
2 slices of ham
2 tablespoons of flour
2 tablespoons of butter
1 tablespoon of sweet paprika
2 tablespoons of marjoram
2 garlic cloves
Black pepper
Pinch of salt

Directions:

1. Boil pea in broth for 30 minutes.
2. Meanwhile fry ham and garlic in butter.
3. Blend the pea with hand blender.
4. Add flour and make roux. Add sweet paprika.
5. Add roux to broth. Add pepper, salt, marjoram and cook for 20 minutes.
6. Serve with fresh bread.

Chłodnik, Cold Borshch

Yield: 8 servings

Ingredients:

5 young, tender beets, with tops
2 cucumbers, peeled and grated
6 radishes, grated
2 green onions, chopped
4 cups plain yogurt
4 cups buttermilk
1 cup sour cream
3 hardboiled eggs, quartered
3 tablespoons dill, chopped
1/2 teaspoon salt
Salt and pepper, to taste

Directions:

1. Prepare the beets by removing and dicing the stems up to the leaves.
2. Add the chopped stems to a large soup pot.
3. Peel and grate the remaining beet roots, add to the pan. Add enough water just to cover the beets, add salt.
4. Simmer until tender, about 15 minutes.
5. Cool the beet mixture.
6. Add the cucumbers, radishes, dill, green onions, yogurt, kefir, and sour cream.
7. Season with salt and pepper.
8. Chill and serve garnished with hardboiled egg.

Kapuśniak, Cabbage Soup

Yield: 4 servings

Ingredients:

400g potatoes
400g sauerkraut
200g sausage
1 onion
1 garlic clove
1 tablespoon sweet paprika
2 tablespoons lad
100g sour cream
1 tablespoon flour
Pinch of salt
Black pepper
Crushed cumin

Directions:

1. Boil diced potatoes with salt and cumin for 20 minutes.
2. Fry diced onion in lard in pan.
3. Add sauerkraut pour 1 liter water and add paprika.
4. Boil for 10 minutes.
5. Meanwhile make roux by frying flour with sour cream.
6. Add sauerkraut roux and cut sausage to the potatoes and cook for 10 minutes.
7. Serve with fresh bread.

Kartoflanka, Potato Soup

Yield: 4 servings

Ingredients:

3 large potatoes
1 small onion
1 sprig of parsley
1 small celery
2 small carrots
2 tablespoons of dried mushrooms
1 garlic clove
2 tablespoons of marjoram
2 tablespoons of oil
2 tablespoons of flour
2 teaspoons of marjoram

Directions:

1. Fry onion, flour and garlic in butter in pot.
2. Add 1,5l water and boil for 5 minutes.
3. Add diced vegetable, mushrooms and boil for 30 minutes.
4. Add salt, pepper, marjoram and boil for 5 minutes.
5. Serve with fresh bread.

Krupnik, Barley Soup

Yield: 8 servings

Ingredients:

500g dried porcini mushrooms
13 cups stock
2 small carrots
2 small turnips
2 small onions
2 medium potatoes
2 stalks celery and leaves
3/4 cup pearl barley
Sour cream

Directions:

1. Soak the cepes in a little water for 15 minutes, until they soften.
2. Chop all the vegetables finely in 2 batches in the food processor and put them in a pan with the barley and all the broth.
3. Chop the softened mushrooms in the food processor, and add them to the pot.
4. Bring to the boil, remove the scum, season with plenty of salt and pepper, and simmer for 1 hour.
5. The barley will thicken the soup.
6. Serve with sour cream.

Rosół, Broth with Noodles

Yield: 6 servings

Ingredients:

1/2 chicken with bones
500g beef with bones
2 carrots
1 parsley root
1 celery
1/2 leek
2 dried mushrooms
1 onion
1 teaspoon of black peppercorns
2 dried bay leaves

Directions:

1. Boil meat in 2 liters of water for 1 hour.
2. Add carrot, parsley, celery, leek, mushrooms and onion. Don't forget to add salt, peppercorns and bay leaves.
3. Boil for an additional hour.
4. Remove meat and vegetable. Slice vegetable and return it back.
5. Serve with noodles.

Zupa Grzybowa, Mushroom Soup

Yield: 8 servings

Ingredients:

3 carrots
2 parsnips
1/2 celery root
1 package of dried mushrooms
1 container of fresh mushrooms
1 piece beef with round bone
1 large onion
4 large potatoes

Directions:

1. Peel and wash all your vegetables. Dice all vegetable.
2. Put the dried mushrooms in a bowl and cover them with boiling water, let them soak for at least half hour.
3. In a large pot filled with water put all your vegetables and beef and salt pepper to taste. Cook until water boils and turn heat to low.
4. In a frying pan fry the fresh mushrooms until golden brown and throw them into the soup. Fry the onions, throw them into the soup.
5. Put the soaked dry mushrooms into the soup with the water they were soaking in. Let it cook for an hour on low heat.
6. At the very end I take out the meat with the bone. Cut the meat into small pieces and throw it back into the soup.
7. When serving sprinkle a pinch of fresh herbs.

Zupa Ogórkowa, Pickle Soup

Yield: 6 servings

Ingredients:

8 cups chicken or vegetable stock
1 pound peeled and quartered potatoes
2 large peeled and diced carrots
1 large peeled and diced parsnip
1 rib diced celery
6 shredded dill pickles
1 cup sour cream
Chopped fresh dill

Directions:

1. In a large saucepan, bring the stock to a boil. Add potatoes, carrots, parsnip and celery. Return to the boil, reduce heat and simmer until vegetables are tender.
2. Add pickles and any accumulated juices and combine well.
3. Temper the sour cream in a small heatproof bowl by adding a few ladles of hot soup and whisking constantly.
4. Transfer the tempered sour cream back to the soup and heat through until starting to simmer but do not boil or the sour cream will break.
5. Serve hot in heated bowls with chopped fresh dill and slices of rye bread with caraway seeds.

Zupa Szczawiowa, Sorrel Soup

Yield: 6 servings

Ingredients:

200g fresh sorrel, washed, stemmed as for spinach and chopped
6 cups cold water
1 large peeled and sliced carrot
1 bunch fresh parsley
1 bay leaf
3 peeled and cubed medium potatoes
1 chicken or vegetable bouillon cube
1 tablespoon butter
1 cup sour cream
1 tablespoon all-purpose flour
Chopped fresh dill or parsley
2 hard-cooked eggs cut into quarters
Salt and pepper to taste

Directions:

1. In a large saucepan place 6 cups cold water, carrots and parsley. Bring to a boil and add bay leaf, potatoes, and bouillon cube. Bring back to a boil, reduce heat and simmer until vegetables are tender.
2. In a large skillet, melt butter and sauté sorrel for 10 minutes. Transfer to the soup and bring to a boil. Reduce heat. Remove bay leaf.
3. In a heatproof bowl or measuring cup, fork blend sour cream with flour and temper with a few ladles of hot soup, whisking constantly until smooth.
4. Transfer tempered sour cream-flour mixture to soup, stir well and simmer until thickened and just under the boiling point. Adjust seasonings.
5. Portion soup into heated bowls and garnish with chopped dill or parsley and egg quarters.

Zupa Tomidorowa, Tomato Soup

Yield: 4 servings

Ingredients:

1l vegetable broth
400g peeled tomatoes
1 can of tomato sauce
4 tablespoons of olive oil
1 onions
4 garlic cloves
2 bay leaf
3 allspice
1 tablespoon of sugar
Black pepper
Pinch of salt
Basil
Cooked pasta

Directions:

1. Fry diced onion in oil.
2. Add garlic. Add peeled tomatoes (whole).
3. Pour vegetable broth and add bay leaf with allspice (best in teabag).
4. Boil for 10 minutes.
5. Remove all spice and blend the soup.
6. Add tomato sauce and sugar.
7. Serve with basil and cooked rice.

Żurek, Rye Soup

Yield: 6 servings

Ingredients:

Kwas:
75g whole meal rye flour
600ml boiled, cooled water
1/4 garlic clove
Soup:
1 1/4 l vegetable stock
100g bacon
100g onions
1 can mushroom
400ml kwas
300ml sour cream
5 medium potatoes, cooked and diced
100g smoked sausage, diced

Directions:

1. Rinse out an earthenware jar or any non-aluminum container with boiling water.
2. Put the flour in the jar and mix to a liquid paste with a little of water. Leave the mixture to settle for a few minutes, and then pour on the remaining boiled water.
3. Chop the garlic and add.
4. Cover the top of the jar with muslin or pierced cling film and leave in a warm place for 4 to 5 days to ferment.
5. Strain and use as required.
6. If stored in an airtight container, it will keep for a few weeks.
7. Heat the stock.
8. Chop bacon and onion and add to stock.
9. Simmer for 10 minutes.
10. Add mushrooms, kwas, cream and garlic. Season with salt and pepper.
11. Allow to simmer for 20 minutes and then add potatoes and sausage.
12. Bring to boil.
13. Served in hollowed bread.

Main Courses

Golabki, Stuffed Cabbage

Bigos

Yield: 5 servings

Ingredients:

1/2 medium cabbage
4 cups of sauerkraut
1 can of tomato paste
500g sliced bacon
500g diced pork meat
500g sliced sausage
1 large onion, diced
2 garlic cloves
1 bay leaf
Salt
Pepper

Directions:

1. Cut your washed cabbage in thin slices and boil until tender in a pot.
2. Boil the sauerkraut in another pot in about 2 cups of water.
3. Strain and keep the sour water aside.
4. Fry your diced pork in a pan then set aside.
5. Fry the bacon and sausage with the onion and garlic.
6. In a large pot, combine the cooked cabbage, sauerkraut, sour water, tomato paste, spices and your cooked meats, onion and garlic.
7. Boil for about 1 hour.
8. Serve.

Golabki, Cabbage Rolls

Yield: 4 servings

Ingredients:

1 head of cabbage
1kg beef mincemeat
1kg pork mincemeat
2 cups of cooked rice
2 eggs
4 garlic cloves
1 large onion
2 tablespoons of butter
2 tablespoons of marjoram
1 teaspoon of marjoram
1 tablespoon of thyme
1 teaspoon of salt
1 teaspoon of pepper
2 cans of crushed tomatoes
1 can of tomato sauce

Directions:

1. Fry minced garlic and chopped onion in butter until golden.
2. Beat 2 eggs with marjoram, thyme, salt, and pepper. In a bowl mix mincemeat, rice, onion, garlic, and eggs. Mix it well. Cover it and let rest in the fridge.
3. Core cabbage.
4. Blanche cabbage leaves in boiling water, peeling them off as they become limp. Once leaves are separated, cut of stems (centers).
5. Put about 2 tablespoons of filling in the center of each leaf.
6. Fold the sides of the leaf in and roll it up into a little package. Put rolls in casserole. Pour rolls with all cans of tomatoes.
7. Sprinkle with marjoram.
8. Bake at 180°C for 2 hours.
9. Serve.

Kaczka z Jabłkami, Duck with Apples

Yield: 6 servings

Ingredients:

Duck
1 1/2 teaspoon salt
1 teaspoon pepper
1/2 teaspoon garlic powder
1/2 teaspoon paprika
5 small apples
1/4 cup honey
1/4 cup fresh orange juice, strained
2 tablespoons lemon juice, strained

Directions:

1. In a small bowl, combine salt, pepper, garlic powder, and paprika.
2. Remove the insides of the duck, then wash and pat it dry. Rub the inside and outside of the duck with the spice and salt mixture.
3. Core the apples and cut them into halves.
4. Stuff the duck as much as possible with the apples. Then tie the drumsticks with kitchen twine.
5. Place the duck upside down into a roasting pan.
6. Whisk together the honey, orange juice, and lemon juice. And glaze the duck.
7. Roast at 180°C for 1 hour.

Klopsiki, Polish Meatballs

Yield: 6 servings

Ingredients:

300g ground beef chuck
200g lean ground pork
1 slice stale white bread
1/4 cup milk
1 small finely chopped onion
1 large slightly beaten egg
2 tablespoons breadcrumbs
2 tablespoons beef stock or water
Salt and pepper to taste
Mushroom Sauce:
40g porcini mushrooms
200g fresh sliced mushrooms
2 tablespoons all-purpose flour
2 cups boiling water
2 tablespoons butter
1 chopped onion
1 teaspoon chicken base
1 cup sour cream
Salt and pepper to taste

Directions:

1. In a large bowl, soak bread in milk until soft. Add beef, pork, onion, egg, salt and pepper, and mix thoroughly. If the mixture feels too mushy, add 1 to 2 tablespoons breadcrumbs. To make sure your seasonings are on point, fry up a tiny patty, taste and adjust as necessary.
2. Heat oven to 150°C. Using a medium cookie scoop, portion out meatballs, giving a final roll with dampened hands.
3. Lightly coat a skillet with cooking spray and brown meatballs on all sides. Transfer to a baking pan with a lip, add 2 tablespoons water or stock and bake, uncovered, 30 minutes.
4. **Sauce:** Place dried mushrooms in a heatproof bowl and pour 2 cups boiling water over. Let steep 1/2 hour.
5. Meanwhile, in a medium saucepan, sauté 1 large chopped onion in butter until caramelized. Add mushrooms to the saucepan once the onions are translucent.
6. Add chicken base. Bring to a boil, reduce heat and simmer, covered, 30 minutes.

7. In a medium bowl, fork blend 2 tablespoons flour into sour cream. Temper the sour cream by adding 3 ladles of hot mushroom liquid, 1 ladle at a time, and whisking until smooth. Slowly pour the tempered sour cream back into the mushroom sauce, whisking constantly.
8. Simmer 5 to 10 minutes until thickened and raw flour taste is cooked out.
9. The cooked meatballs can be immersed in this sauce, reheated and served over noodles, mashed potatoes or rice.

Kotlet Mielony

Yield: 4 servings

Ingredients:

500g minced meat
5 garlic cloves
100ml water
1 onion
Flour
Breadcrumbs
Marjoram
Cumin
Parsley
Black pepper
Oil
Salt

Directions:

1. Mix meat with water and leave it for 30 minutes.
2. Dice onion.
3. Add onion, egg, pepper, cumin, marjoram, garlic, parsley, salt, flour and breadcrumbs. Mix it well and shape small flattened balls.
4. Fry in oil on both sides.
5. Serve with potatoes.

Kotlet Schabowy

Yield: 4 servings

Ingredients:

4 medium pork chops
60g flour
1/4 teaspoon garlic powder
1/4 teaspoon dried marjoram
1 egg, beaten
1 tablespoon oil
1 tablespoon butter
Salt and pepper

Directions:

1. Pound out the pork chops until fairly thin. Season with salt, pepper, garlic powder and marjoram. Set aside.
2. On separate plates, pour flour and egg.
3. Dip each chop into the flour, coating on both sides, and then dip into the beaten egg. Then back into flour, ensuring even coating.
4. Heat oil and butter in a large frying pan. When very hot, add the pork and cook over high heat for 3-5 minutes on each side.
5. Lower heat and cook for another few minutes until golden.
6. Serve with cooked potatoes.

Łosoś Pieczony, Baked Salmon

Yield: 2 servings

Ingredients:

2 salmon fillets, boneless, without skin
2 garlic cloves
30g butter
1 tablespoon chopped fresh dill
1/2 teaspoon crushed black peppercorns
1 tablespoon lemon juice
1 tablespoon water/stock/dry white wine
1 bay leaf, deveined and snipped in slices
Salt

Directions:

1. Preheat oven to 200°C.
2. Wash and pat the salmon dry and place skin side down, in the middle of an aluminum foil large enough to fold over in a slight tent shape.
3. Place all the other ingredients in a bowl and mix thoroughly.
4. Spread the paste on one fillet and place the other fillet over it.
5. Pull both sides of the foil up and seal top and sides, leaving a little space at the top for the salmon to steam.
6. Bake in the oven for 20-25 minutes.
7. Serve with potatoes and cucumber salad.

Paszteciki

Yield: 8 servings

Ingredients:

1 cup flour
1/8 teaspoon salt
1 hard-boiled egg, yolk only
1 egg
5 tablespoons unsalted butter, softened
Filling:
6 tablespoons unsalted butter, softened
200g beef brisket, cooked, trimmed of fat & cut into 1-inch pieces
1/3 cup onion, chopped
1/2 cup rutabaga, diced
2 eggs, lightly beaten separately
1 teaspoon salt
1/4 teaspoon pepper

Directions:

1. Sift flour and salt into a large mixing bowl. Use a spoon to push the egg yolk through a fine sieve into the flour.
2. Add the raw egg and mix well. Beat in butter 1 tablespoon at a time.
3. Place dough on a floured surface and knead until smooth and elastic, then wrap in waxed paper and refrigerate until firm.
4. In a heavy skillet, melt 2 tablespoons butter over medium heat, sauté the onion and rutabaga until the onion is soft and transparent
5. Put the onions, rutabaga, and beef through a meat grinder twice if you have one, if not just chop them up as fine as possible.
6. Melt the remaining 4 tablespoons butter over medium heat, and add the meat mixture. Cook over low heat, stirring occasionally, until all of the liquid has evaporated and the mixture is thick enough to hold its shape.
7. Remove from heat and let cool, then stir in 1 egg, and season with salt and pepper.
8. Preheat oven to 170°C.
9. On a lightly floured surface, roll the dough out into a thin rectangle. Cut the rectangle into smaller ones. Spoon the filling down the center of the rectangle lengthwise, leaving about an inch of space on each end.
10. Lightly brush the long sides with cold water, then fold one of the long sides over the filling and the other side over the top of that.

11. Brush the short ends with cold water and fold them over the top, enclosing the filling.
12. Place pastry seam side down on a baking sheet and brush the top evenly with the remaining scrambled egg.
13. Bake in preheated oven until rich golden brown, 30 minutes.

Pierogi with Cheese Filling

Yield: 4 servings

Ingredients:

3 cups of flour
3 tablespoons of oil
1 cup of warm water
Filling:
8 boiled diced large potatoes
1 chopped onion
2 cups of cheese (similar to Cheddar)
Salt

Directions:

1. Mix flour, water and oil to make dough. Make small squares from dough.
2. Put potatoes with onion and cheese in a bowl. Mash it to make thick mixture.
3. Place a scoop of the filling in the middle of each square and fold them.
4. Press edges with fork.
5. Boil them in salt water for 10 minutes.
6. Serve topped with chopped chive, fried onion, cream and salad.

Placki Ziemniaczane, Potato Pancakes

Yield: 5 servings

Ingredients:

1kg potatoes
2 eggs
4 tablespoons of flour
4 garlic cloves
4 handfuls of marjoram
Lard
Pepper
Salt

Directions:
1. Grate cooked potatoes in the bowl. Mix them with egg, flour, garlic, salt, pepper and marjoram. Make dough.
2. Melt lard in pan. Form pancakes and fry until golden.
3. Serve.

Polish Goulash

Yield: 4 servings

Ingredients:

100g salami
250g sausage
2 onions
2 tablespoons of sweet paprika
1kg potatoes
1 tablespoon of crushed cumin
50ml oil
125ml cooking cream
Salt

Directions:

1. Cook boil potatoes.
2. Meanwhile fry onion in oil.
3. Add diced potatoes, spice, salt, sliced sausage, salami and fry it for a while.
4. Pour some water, add salt and boil for 30 minutes.
5. Serve with fresh bread, dumplings or potato pancakes

Pyzy, Meat Stuffed Potato Dumplings

Yield: 4 servings

Ingredients:

250g smoked meat
100g cottage cheese
700g potatoes
150g flour
80g breadcrumbs
100g semolina
1 onion
2 eggs
Oil
Salt
Sauerkraut

Directions:

1. Boil meat for 1 hour and potatoes for 30 minutes.
2. Dice meat and fry with onion in oil.
3. Peel and grate potatoes. Mix them with breadcrumbs, flour, semolina, salt and whipped eggs. Make a dough and roll it 1cm thick. Cut squares.
4. Mix meat, onion and cheese. Spoon the mixture in the middle of each one and make dumplings.
5. Boil them in salt water for 20 minutes.
6. Serve with sauerkraut and fried onion.

Zrazy

Yield: 5 servings

Ingredients:

1kg top round steaks, trimmed of fat and pounded to 1/4 inch thick
700g mushrooms, finely chopped
5 tablespoons of unsalted butter
3 tablespoons of vegetable oil
3 cups of onions, finely chopped
1/4 cup of breadcrumbs
1 teaspoon of salt
1/2 teaspoon of pepper
2 teaspoons of mustard
3 tablespoons of flour
1 cup of beef broth
2/3 cup of sour cream

Directions:

1. Melt 2 tablespoons butter with 1 tablespoon oil in pan. Fry mushrooms and onions for 10 minutes.
2. Stir in the bread crumbs and half of the salt and pepper; remove from heat.
3. Cut the steak into 8 rectangular pieces 4 inch wide by 8 inch long, sprinkle both sides evenly with remaining salt and pepper. Spread a thin layer of the mustard on each slice of beef, and place 1/8 of the stuffing on the shorter end of each piece of steak.
4. Roll the steaks into rolls, enclosing the stuffing, and tuck in the sides; secure each end with kitchen cord.
5. Cover the rolls in flour.
6. In another pan melt remaining butter and oil.
7. Fry rolls until rich golden, 15 minutes.
8. Transfer them to casserole.
9. Clean the pan. Pour in broth and boil over high heat.
10. Pour the broth over rolls in casserole. Bake it for 45 minutes.
11. Remove rolls and pour liquid, try to discard as much fat as you can, from casserole in pan. Boil over high heat. Remove from heat and mix in sour cream.
12. Serve topped with sauce.

Desserts

Sernik, Polish Cheesecake

Budyn, Vanilla Pudding

Yield: 3 servings

Ingredients:

2 cups milk
1 tablespoon butter
3 tablespoon vanilla sugar
1/2 vanilla pod
2 tablespoon potato starch
2 egg yolks

Directions:

1. Bring 1 1/2 cup of milk, butter, vanilla sugar and scraped vanilla seeds to a boil.
2. Mix the remaining milk with egg yolks and potato starch until smooth. Add it into the boiling milk and lower the heat.
3. Boil another minute or until the mixture thickens.
4. Pour it into glass bowls.
5. Decorate it with chocolate, chopped nuts, or fruits.
6. Refrigerate for an hour.
7. Serve

Faworki

Yield: 10 servings

Ingredients:

2 1/2 cups all-purpose flour
6 egg yolks
3 tablespoons sour cream
2 tablespoons white sugar
2 tablespoons butter, softened
1 tablespoon rum
1 pinch salt
2 cups vegetable oil for frying
1/2 cup confectioners' sugar

Directions:

1. Combine flour, egg yolks, sour cream, sugar, butter, rum, and salt in a large bowl; mix to form a dough.
2. Knead dough lightly and roll out on a floured surface. Cut into strips 4 inches long and 3/4 inches wide. Cut a slit in the middle of each strip. Twist and pull one end through the slit.
3. Heat oil in a deep-fryer or large saucepan. Test the temperature by dropping in a pastry twist; the oil is ready when it browns and float to the surface.
4. Fry pastry twists in batches until golden brown, about 1 minute per side. Drain on a plate lined with paper towels. Dust with confectioners' sugar.

Chalka, Jewish Challah

Ingredients:

8 teaspoons of active yeast
2 tablespoons of sugar
5 cup of water
1 and half cups of honey
2 tablespoons of salt
1 and quarter cups of oil
1 egg
2.2kg all-purpose flour
Topping:
1 cup of flour
1 cup of sugar
Half a cup of olive oil
1 teaspoon of vanilla extract

Directions:

1. Mix 1 cup of water, sugar and yeast. When it bubbles add honey, salt oil and egg. Mix it well.
2. Add remaining water and flour. Make dough. Let dough rise for 2 hours.
3. Split dough into 6 pieces and that 6 into 6 smaller ones. And braid challahs.
4. Let challah rise for 20 minutes. Brush them with egg wash.
5. Bake challahs for 45 minutes at 180°C.
6. Mix all topping ingredients and sprinkle it the mixture over challahs.
7. Serve cooled.

Kissel

Yield: 5 servings

Ingredients:

400g crushed strawberries
1 cup water
1/2 cup sugar
3 tablespoons potato starch
4 tablespoons cornstarch
1/2 cup cold water

Directions:

1. In a large saucepan, bring to boil 1 cup water and sugar. Remove from heat.
2. Dissolve potato starch in 1/2 cup cold water and stir into the sugar-water mixture. Return to the heat and bring to a boil, stirring constantly. Add strawberries and mix well.
3. Portion into individual dessert bowls or one large bowl that has been rinsed with cold water. Place in the refrigerator until firm, about 3 hours. Serve with cream, half-and-half, milk or whipped cream.

Makoviec

Yield: 10 servings

Ingredients:

30g yeast
320g flour
4 tablespoons of sugar
1/4 teaspoon of salt
1 tablespoon of strong alcohol
3/4 teaspoon of vanilla extract
4 egg yolks
120ml milk
100g butter
Filling:
330g poppy seeds
112g light brown sugar
65g raisins
33g walnuts, chopped
2 tablespoons of honey
1 teaspoons of almond extract
1/2 teaspoons of cinnamon
1/2 tablespoons of butter,
1/3 cup of candied orange zest
4 egg whites

Directions:

1. Mix yeast with 1 tablespoon of sugar. Add 2 tablespoons of flour and all milk, stir and leave aside for 20-30 minutes.
2. Add remaining flour, alcohol, vanilla extract, egg yolks and milk and knead until well combined (around 5-10 minutes).
3. Add melted butter and knead until well mixed. Cover the dough with a tea towel and leave it to rise in a warm place for an hour.
4. **Filling:** Place poppy seeds in a medium bowl and pour boiling water over it. Leave it to cool. Remove the access of water and ground it in a coffee grinder twice.
5. Add sugar, raisins, walnuts, honey, almond extract, cinnamon, butter, candied orange zest and mix it well. In a separate bowl whip egg whites.
6. Add it into poppy seed mixture and gently fold it in.

7. Divide the dough in two. Roll each part of the dough on a floured surface.
8. Spread the filling on each of the rectangles.
9. Starting at the long edge, roll the dough like a roll. Turn ends under so filling will not leak out.
10. Bake rolls at 190°C for 40 minutes.
11. Leave them to cool. Serve.

Mazurek, Flat Cake

Yield: 6 servings

Ingredients:

180g room-temperature butter
4 tablespoons sugar
50g ground blanched almonds
1/2 teaspoon grated lemon zest
2 1/2 cups all-purpose flour
2 large hard-cooked egg yolks, sieved
1 large raw egg yolk
180g apricot preserves
180g raspberry or cherry preserves
Confectioners' sugar
Pinch salt
Pinch cinnamon

Directions:

1. Cream together butter and sugar with an electric mixer until light and fluffy. By hand, stir in almonds, zest, flour, making sure to measure flour correctly, and hard-cooked egg yolks.
2. Add raw egg yolk, salt and cinnamon, and mix into a smooth dough. This entire process, from step 1, can be done in a food processor, if you prefer.
3. Place dough in plastic wrap and refrigerate for at least 30 minutes.
4. Heat oven to 180°C.
5. Cut off 1/3 dough and return, wrapped, to the refrigerator. Roll out 2/3 dough and place on a tart pan. Pierce or "dock" the dough with the tines of a fork. Using pastry brush, egg wash (1 beaten egg with 1 teaspoon water) dough.
6. Roll remaining 1/3 dough and cut into strips. Arrange strips lattice-style over dough. Brush lattice strips with egg wash. Bake for 20 to 30 minutes, or until light golden brown and crisp.
7. Allow to cool completely. Place pastry on a serving plate and spoon fruit preserves alternately into the open spaces of the lattice work. Sprinkle lightly with confectioners' sugar.

Pączki, Doughnuts

Yield: 6 servings

Ingredients:

1kg flour
500ml milk
100g coarse flour
2 tablespoons of granulated sugar
100g butter
5 yolks
70g yeast
1 tablespoon of lemon peel
Yeast
Vanilla sugar
5 tablespoons of rum
Jam as filling
Salt

Directions:

1. Mix 100 milliliters of milk, sugar and yeast. Leave it for 10 minutes in warm room.
2. Mix butter, sugar and rum together. Add vanilla sugar and lemon peel. Add flour and leaven. Make dough.
3. Leave it in the dark for 1 hour.
4. Make pancakes and place filling in the middle and roll it to a dumpling shape.
5. Let doughnuts stay for 30 minutes.
6. Heat oil and deep fry doughnuts.
7. Leave them to cool down, serve.

Sernik, Polish Cheesecake

Yield: 10 servings

Ingredients:

1 1/2 cups flour
1 teaspoon baking powder
1/3 cup sugar
1/4 teaspoon salt
1/4 cup unsalted butter, chilled
1 egg
1/4 cup sour cream or 1/4 cup plain yogurt
Filling:
6 eggs, separated
2 cups sugar
1 teaspoon vanilla extract
6 tablespoons unsalted butter, softened
1 1/2 cups mashed potatoes
400g farmer's cheese
1/4 cup limoncello
2 teaspoons baking powder
1/2 teaspoon fresh grated nutmeg
1/2 teaspoon salt
1 lemon zest

Directions:

1. Preheat oven to 170°C.
2. Pulse flour, baking powder, sugar, and salt in a food processor and butter and pulse till crumbly. Add egg and sour cream mix till it comes to a ball.
3. With heavy floured hands press into a cake mold.
4. Beat egg whites in a mixer till stiff, set aside.
5. Beat egg yolks, sugar and vanilla till light and creamy.
6. In a food processor place butter, potatoes, cheese, Grand Marnier or limoncello, nutmeg, salt and zest of lemon or orange pulse till all combined.
7. Add to yolk mixture folding in to incorporate.
8. Fold in beaten egg whites.
9. Pour onto crust.
10. Bake for 50 minutes.
11. Serve cooled.

Side Dishes

Kopytka, Potato Dumplings

Ćwikla

Yield: 4 servings

Ingredients:

400g beets, cooked, peeled, cooled and grated
1 teaspoon white vinegar
1 teaspoon brown sugar
2 cups horseradish
1/4 teaspoon salt

Directions:

1. In a large bowl, mix together vinegar, brown sugar, horseradish, and salt until well combined. Add beets and mix thoroughly.
2. Pack into clean sterilized jars and store refrigerated for up to 2 weeks.
3. Serve warm or cold, although cold is more traditional.

Kopytka, Potato Dumplings

Yield: 6 servings

Ingredients:

500g potatoes, peeled
250g plain flour
1 egg, beaten
1 large sweet onion, finely chopped
200g chanterelle mushrooms
Olive oil
Butter
Sea salt and ground black pepper

Directions:

1. Boil the potatoes in a large pan of salted water until very soft. Drain and set to one side to cool down and steam dry. Once cool, mash until smooth.
2. Put the cold mashed potato into a large bowl. Add the flour, egg and a good pinch of salt and pepper. Using a metal spoon, bring the mixture together. Knead it until all the flour is incorporated into the potato. The dough should come together and be fairly soft and springy, but not be too sticky.
3. Sprinkle some extra flour onto the board and cut the dough into four quarters. Roll each piece into a long cylinder and cut at an angle into one-inch pieces. Repeat until you have used up all the dough.
4. Bring a fresh pan of salted water to the boil and drop a few dumplings in at a time. When they rise, remove them.
5. Take a large frying pan and add one tablespoon of oil and a good knob of butter. Fry the chopped sweet onions until translucent.
6. Add the dumplings and fry until they turn golden. Throw in the mushrooms and cook for a further couple of minutes. Serve with a scattering of fresh parsley.

Mizeria, Cucumber Salad

Yield: 10 servings

Ingredients:

400h small cucumbers, peeled and thinly sliced
1 bunch dill, chopped
2 1/2 tablespoons sour cream
1 teaspoon lemon juice
1 pinch white sugar
Salt and black pepper to taste

Directions:

1. Sprinkle salt over cucumbers in a bowl. Let stand until cucumbers are soft, about 5 minutes. Squeeze liquid from cucumbers and discard. Add dill to cucumbers.
2. Mix sour cream, lemon juice, and sugar in a bowl; add to cucumbers and toss to coat. Season with black pepper. Chill completely before serving, at least 30 minutes.

Tłuczone Ziemniaki, Mashed Potatoes

Yield: 6 servings

Ingredients:

6 large potatoes
250ml milk (or sour cream)
25g butter
Crushed cumin
Salt
Optionally: fried diced bacon

Directions:

1. Boil peeled diced potatoes for 30 minutes.
2. Meanwhile heat up the milk. Strain the water, add butter and mash potatoes while pouring milk.

Volume Conversion

Customary Quantity	Metric Equivalent
1 teaspoon	5 ml
1 tablespoon	15 ml
1/8 cup	30 ml
1/4 cup	60 ml
1/3 cup	80 ml
1/2 cup	120 ml
2/3 cup	160 ml
3/4 cup	180 ml
1 cup	240 ml
1 1/2 cups	360 ml
2 cups	480 ml
3 cups	720 ml
4 cups	960 ml

Weights of Common Ingredients

Ingredient	1 cup	1/2 cup	2 Tbs
Flour	120 g	70 g	15 g
Sugar	200 g	100 g	25 g
Rice	190 g	100 g	24 g
Macaroni	140 g	70 g	17 g
Butter	240 g	120 g	30 g
Chopped Nuts	150 g	75 g	20 g
Bread Crumbs	150 g	75 g	20 g
Grated Cheese	90 g	45 g	11 g

Temperature Conversion

Fahrenheit	Celsius
250	120
275	140
300	150
325	160
c350	180
375	190
400	200
425	220
450	203

Length Conversion

Inch	cm
0,125	0,32
0,25	0,63
0,5	1,27
1	2,54
2	5,08
5	12,7

Thank you, my reader, for investing time and money to read this book!

The stores all full of many books dedicated to cooking either collecting and sharing recipes or presenting new ones. I sincerely thank you for choosing this very book and reading it to its very end.

I hope you have enjoyed this book as much as possible and that you have learnt something new and interesting. If you have enjoyed this book, please take a few minutes to write a review summarizing your thoughts and opinion on this book.

If you are interested in other paperback books of mine check out my official amazon author's profile:

www.amazon.com/author/prochazkacook

Besides printed book Amazon offers eBook as well, but if you do not enjoy Amazon's Kindle, my books can be found in other stores such as Kobo.com, Lulu.com, or even iBook for Apple devices.

Thanks for buying this books and have best of luck.

Sincerely,

Lukas Prochazka

Learn more about Slavic cuisines

If you are interested in other Slavic countries you should consider checking out the other Slavic cookbooks.

Czech cuisine is regarded as one of the best cuisine by the experts yet it gets little attention. Learn how to make genuine Czech meals.

If you want to learn more about Czech pubs and the meal served in those, check out the Czech Pub Food cookbook.

Eastern Europe is dominated by Slavic culture. No cuisine is more diverse in its taste then Slavic one. Learn genuine Slavic recipes of the major Slavic countries.

Made in the USA
Las Vegas, NV
20 November 2023

81200834R00037